ANIMAL EMOTIONS

WHEN CATS GET ANGRY

HEATHER MOORE NIVER

Enslow Publishing
101 W. 23rd Street
Suite 240
New York, NY 10011
USA
enslow.com

WORDS TO KNOW

body language Communication using the body's movements instead of words.

domesticated An animal that becomes tame; kept in a home or on a farm.

feline dwarfism A condition in cats that results in short legs.

imitation Something that copies something else.

neurotransmitters Materials that transport nerve impulses.

predator An animal that hunts, or preys on, other animals.

prey An animal tracked and killed for food by another animal.

pupil The dark circle in the center of the eye.

subtle Not obvious.

territory An area defended by an animal.

CONTENTS

CHAPTER ONE

GRUMPY CAT

You could probably recognize this cat anywhere. Grumpy Cat has a naturally downturned mouth that makes her look angry all the time. It is this expression that has brought her fame. People use Grumpy Cat's face all over the Internet to show when they are feeling cranky.

She has been on television shows like *Good Morning America*. She has two books published under

Finicky Feline: Morris

Morris the Cat is an orange striped celebrity cat. He began appearing in 9 Lives cat food commercials in 1969. Morris starred in more than fifty television commercials and the movie *Shamus* with actor Burt Reynolds.

her name. She has a movie, *Grumpy Cat's Worst Christmas Ever.* She even has her own line of clothing, so you can buy Grumpy Cat socks if you like. Millions of Grumpy Cat fans follow her on Facebook and Instagram.

Grumpy Cat's frowns have made her famous for being unhappy. Our feline friends are often thought of as angry.

Fact

Cats were first kept as pets, or domesticated, about ten thousand years ago.

Grumpy Cat is a two-year-old kitty whose real name is Tardar Sauce. But she is not as out-of-sorts as she seems. In real life, Tardar Sauce is not that angry. She has a disease called **feline dwarfism**. This disease makes her mouth turn down so that she always seems to be pouting.

Cats are known for being independent and even angry. But what makes these fuzzy friends angry? Keep reading to find out more about cat emotions.

CHAPTER TWO

PURRING AND OTHER CAT MYSTERIES IN HISTORY

Scientist Charles Darwin thought that animal minds were a lot like human minds. In 1871, he wrote that he thought that many animals felt emotions, "such as love, memory, attention, curiosity, **imitation**, reason." These are feelings that people feel every day.

One of the biggest mysteries about cats has gone on for about three thousand years! Why do cats purr?

The First Cats

Experts believe that the first domesticated cats were most likely kept as pets in the Middle East. Today cats are one of the most popular pets on Earth.

But it has not been studied much since the 1970s. For many years it was assumed that a purring cat was a happy cat.

But cats meow in different ways to communicate. They meow when they are hungry, want to get your attention, or are afraid. They may purr for different reasons, too. They purr when they are happy, but they also do so when injured or are giving birth.

Have you heard about cats having "nine lives"? Scientists are studying whether purring has a healing effect on

Cats have the amazing ability to land on their feet. It's one reason why they supposedly have nine lives.

cats. A cat's bones seem to heal more easily and faster than a dog's bones. Many cats also survive falls from great heights. It may be that purring has something to do with survival. Domestic cats and some wild cats—pumas, ocelots, caracals, servals, and cheetahs—all purr.

Fact

All cats, from the fierce lion to the housecat, are related to the clouded leopard.

CHAPTER THREE

CLUES TO AN ANGRY CAT

Want to know what mood your cat is in? Watch its **body language**. This means how it holds its body, face, and even tail. It's much more difficult to figure out a cat's body language than a dog's. This is because cats are **subtler**, or not as obvious. Dogs have very expressive faces, but cats do not.

A cat has other ways of showing you how it feels. When a cat is angry, it will let you know. For

The Truth About Cats and Dogs

Dog emotions seem easier to figure out than cat emotions. It could be because dogs have been human pets for thirty thousand years. Maybe we just know each other better.

example, if your cat hisses, it is warning you. It is trying to tell you that it is unhappy, scared, or getting angry.

A hiss is a warning from your cat! Pay attention, because a hiss means Mittens wants to communicate with you.

It seems to be easier to figure out Fido's feelings, especially compared to cats!

If a cat's hissing gets louder and more intense, look out! It may go on to growl, shriek, scratch, swat, claw, bite, and fight. All of these reactions are to tell you or another animal to leave them alone. This angry cat is likely to start a fight if it is not left alone.

Fact

Never try to touch, comfort, or scold a cat when it is hissing. If the hissing gets louder, back off.

Are the cat's ears flattened toward its back? Look at its eyes. Are its **pupils** small? And is the cat's fur standing on end? These are more signs that your cat is angry.

CHAPTER FOUR

THE BRAINS OF CATS

Compared to dogs and humans, cats have small brains. A cat's brain makes up 0.9 percent of its body. Human brains make up about 2 percent of their bodies. Dog brains make up about 1.2 percent. But cats and humans have very similar brains in some ways. They look the same. The way they are made up is a lot alike.

I Can Read Your Mind

We spend a lot of time trying to read our cats' minds. Scientists now think that cats can know what we are thinking! It appears that cats can tell how we are feeling based on our facial expressions.

Cats' brains can move information quickly, which helps cats make fast decisions.

A cat's brain has two main parts. Each part has a job to do. The two parts have many connections and can share information very quickly. Moving information this quickly helps a cat take in the world around it and decide how to react.

Cats use their whiskers to sense even the smallest movements in the air. What a cool cat tool!

Neurotransmitters are what move information in the brain. These are also alike in humans and cats. Cats use their five senses—sight, smell, hearing, taste, and touch—to process the world around them. Cats have an extra tool, though. Their whiskers are very sensitive. Whiskers can pick up a tiny movement in the air and send information to the brain.

> **Fact**
>
> **Your cat's brain can store one thousand times more data and work one million times faster than a tablet!**

The part of the brain that is in charge of emotions is almost exactly alike in cats and humans! Cats have great memories. They can remember things that happened up to sixteen hours before.

CHAPTER FIVE

ON THE HUNT

It has not been easy for scientists to understand what makes a cat tick. Unlike dogs, cats are famous for refusing to do what humans ask them to do. But we do know a few things about the mysterious minds of cats.

Cats are naturally fantastic hunters, thanks to their great vision and hearing. You might see your cat hunting bugs in the house. Have you ever seen your cat stare outside through the window? You might have noticed your cat becoming extremely focused. The end of her tail twitches. She starts to make an odd, high-

A Mind of Its Own

Scientists have trouble getting cats to do what they want them to do. But when they cooperate, studies show that cats perform almost as well as dogs.

pitched noise. Those are signs your cat is in hunt mode. She is a **predator** eyeing her **prey**. And she'd love to get out there and hunt!

Sometimes it might seem like your cat acts angry for no reason. She might even bite out of the blue. This is called "redirected" anger. A cat may be extremely upset

Does Snowball ever swat or bite out of the blue? Maybe another cat she saw outside upset her.

If your cat's ears are flat and to the side, she may be feeling aggressive.

by something it cannot reach, like looking through the window to see another cat walking across the yard. A while later, even as much as thirty minutes, a human might approach and the cat lashes out! Scientists think this is a reflex, or something done without thinking.

Fact

A new person might smell like other animals, which can cause a cat to get angry.

CHAPTER SIX

HISSY FITS

Cats don't only hiss when they are angry. Cats may hiss if a new cat is in their **territory**. They like their space, and they may feel threatened when another animal is there.

A cat's hiss sounds like a snake. This is called imitation. The hiss may be a warning to back off. A snake's hiss signals that there is a dangerous animal

Halting the Hiss

Give a hissing cat space to relax and calm down. Talk calmly and lovingly. If a strange person is the cause of the hissing, give your cat some of his or her clothing. This helps it get used to the new human's smell.

Cats may hiss at unfamiliar people. Letting your cat sniff at a new person's clothes helps it get to know the person's smells.

around and you should be alert! Even if the cat hisses out of fright, it wants to suggest that it is not afraid to attack. Usually, a cat would rather not fight.

A new cat in your house or the neighborhood might make a cat act out. She will worry about the safety of her food and toys. She will also worry about

Like these lynx, housecats also hiss when another cat is in their space.

Fact

A mother hisses if she's worried about her kittens' safety.

having your love all to herself or that the new cat will start a fight! She might start to hiss. Other reasons for hissing are a new person in the house or an unfamiliar experience, like a new vacuum cleaner that sounds different than the one she is used to.

Rescue cats that were in a shelter or had been in many homes may hiss. They hiss because so many new things are scary.

CHAPTER SEVEN

MOOD CLUES

Cats show many emotions. You just have to know what to look for. Their tails offer some clues. Is he twitching his tail? He's troubled. The faster he lashes it back and forth, the more upset he is. If his tail is straight and his fur is smooth, he is probably happy or interested in what you're doing.

Beware if his tail is twice its usual size! When his hair stands on end, he is angry or upset. Cats hold

Too Rough

If you're playing with your cat and she begins to growl, it's time to calm down. Sometimes play can get too rough for cats. Then they may bite or scratch even the most loved humans.

Fact

If a cat's tail is straight up in the air and shivering, he might be very excited.

their tails low or even between their legs if they are very nervous or worried.

Ears that are flat and backward or sideways are a

A cat tail that suddenly looks very big communicates, "Watch out!" Midnight is very upset about something.

warning. They show that the cat is angry, stressed, or scared. If her ears are moving all around, she is curious and listening to everything around her. She keeps her ears forward when she is happy.

Never try to pet a cat when its back is arched and its hair is standing on end. Growling means it is downright angry.

An arched back can mean a couple of things. If a cat's fur is also standing on end, he might be angry or scared. Smooth fur means you can probably pet him or scratch him between the ears. If he's lying on his back and purring, he is probably relaxed. But if he is growling, back off. He is mad and might be ready to defend himself.

CHAPTER EIGHT

WHEN CATS FEEL LOVE

Cats are a lot like us when it comes to expressing emotions. For example, when someone we know isn't feeling well, we want to help. Cats do that, too. One kitten sensed his owner wasn't feeling well and curled up against his face. His owner was suffering from a toothache!

Some cats even give gifts to their humans. They bring them household items, like hair bands or toys. Other cats bring dead animals to the door. What

Not So Selfish

Dogs wag their tails and follow humans around to show love. Cats don't always do this. But that does not mean they are selfish. They may not show love until they feel like it.

seems gross and yucky to us is a sign of affection in the eyes of a cat.

Cats even seem to feel love. When we are around people we love, we relax and let our guard down. Sometimes cats roll on their backs and expose their furry bellies.

Fact

Be careful when reaching out to give a furry kitty belly a rub. Not all cats enjoy it.

Sometimes Tigger will bring you presents in the form of toys. A dead mouse symbolizes your cat's love, too!

A relaxed cat rolls on its back. Letting you rub their belly shows that they love and trust you.

They only do this when they feel relaxed. Cats only sit next to or on people they completely trust.

Just like humans, not all cats are alike. Cats have different personalities and show their emotions in their own ways, too. Some are very obvious with their affection. Other cats are not as interested in showing their love so clearly.

LEARN MORE

Books

Edwards, Alan, and Trevor Turner. *The Ultimate Encyclopedia of Cats, Cat Breeds & Cat Care*. London, UK: Hermes House, 2014.

Miller, Kelly. *Just Joking: Cats*. Washington, DC: National Geographic, 2016.

Newman, Aline Alexander, and Gary Weitzman. *How to Speak Cat: A Guide to Decoding Cat Language*. Washington, DC: National Geographic, 2015.

Websites

Cat Tail Wagging: What Different Wags Mean

pawculture.com/tips-advice/cat-behavior/cat-tail-wagging-what-different-wags-mean

Learn about how a cat communicates using its tail!

Pets: Cats

animalplanet.com/pets/cats

Photos, facts, and videos all about one of the world's most popular pets: cats!

Question: Why And How Do Cats Purr?

loc.gov/rr/scitech/mysteries/catspurr.html

Learn more about the reasons behind why cats purr.

INDEX

Published in 2018 by Enslow Publishing, LLC.
101 W. 23rd Street, Suite 240, New York, NY 10011

Library of Congress Cataloging-in-Publication Data

Names: Niver, Heather Moore, author.
Title: When cats get angry / Heather Moore Niver.
Description: New York, NY : Enslow Publishing LLC, 2018. | Series: Animal emotions | Includes bibliographical references and index. | Audience: Grades 3 to 5.
Identifiers: LCCN 2016057794| ISBN 9780766088658 (pbk. book : alk. paper) | ISBN 9780766086111 (library bound book : alk. paper) | ISBN 9780766088597 (6 pack : alk. paper)
Subjects: LCSH: Cats–Behavior–Juvenile literature. | Cats–Psychology–Juvenile literature. | Emotions in animals–Juvenile literature.
Classification: LCC SF446.5 .N58 2017 | DDC 636.8/0835–dc23
LC record available at https://lccn.loc.gov/2016057794

Printed in the United States of America

Photo Credits: Cover, p. 1 Nedim Bajramovic/Shutterstock.com; p. 5 Bruce Glikas/FilmMagic/Getty Images; p. 8 Auscape/Universal Images Group/Getty Images; p. 11 ILonika/Shutterstock.com; p. 12 Kellymmiller73/Shutterstock.com; p. 15 Denise Grabowski/EyeEm/Getty Images; p. 16 Ingram Publishing/Thinkstock; p. 19 Torbjörn Larsson/EyeEm/Getty Images; p. 20 ullstein bild/Getty Images; p. 22 David Troncoso/Photolibrary/Getty Images; p. 23 VitalyEdush/iStock/Thinkstock; p. 26 GlobalP/iStock/Thinkstock; p. 27 Astrid860/iStock/Thinkstock; p. 29 Purple Collar Pet Photography/Moment/Getty Images; p. 30 Africa Studio/Shutterstock.com; back cover, interior pages background De Space Studio/Shutterstock.com; interior pages border element Somsak Sarabua/Shutterstock.com